THIS WAY TO BETTER SPEECH

This Way to Better Speech

by

Louise Abney and **Dorothy Miniace**

Chairman, Department of Speech, Teachers College of Kansas City, Missouri Director of Speech Improvement, Kansas City Public Schools

Speech Teacher, Ashland Elementary School, Kansas City, Missouri

World Book Company
Yonkers-on-Hudson, New York

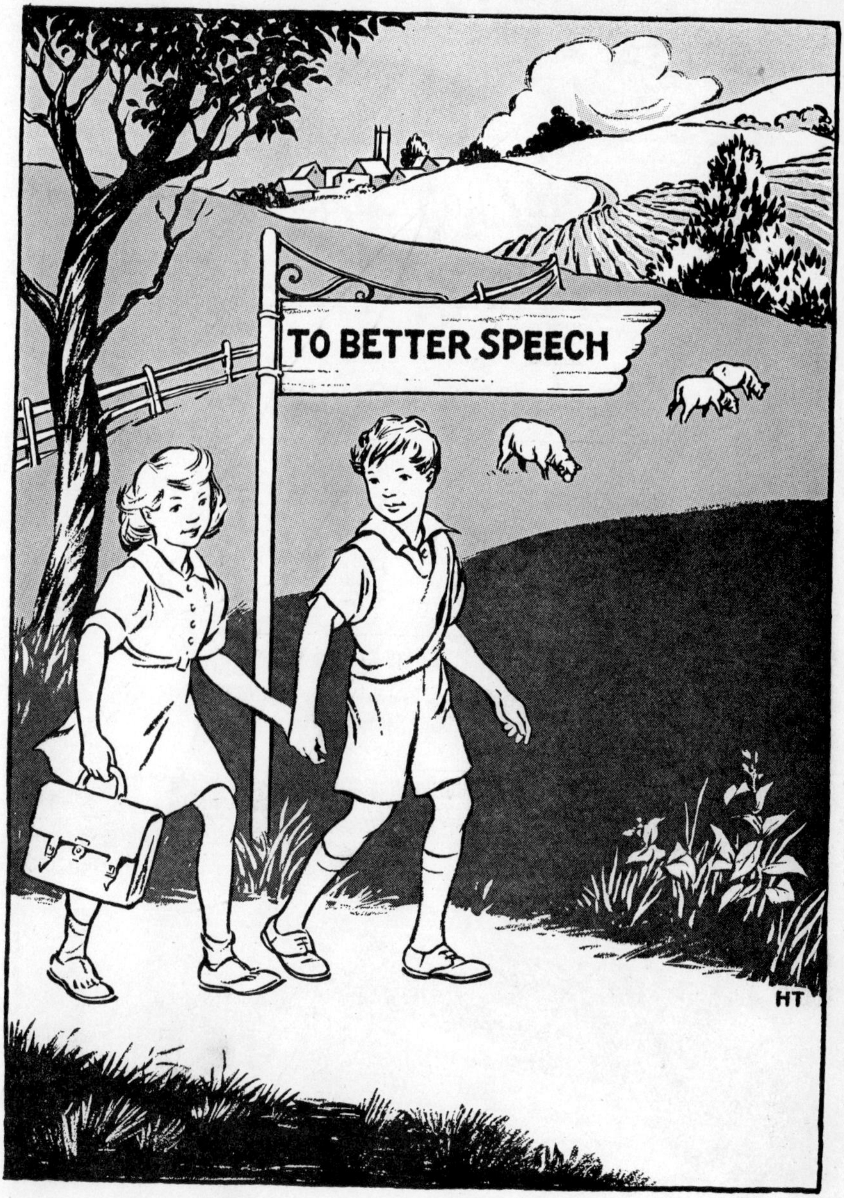
TO BETTER SPEECH
HT

WORLD BOOK COMPANY
The House of Applied Knowledge

Established 1905 by Caspar W. Hodgson

YONKERS–ON–HUDSON, NEW YORK
2126 Prairie Avenue, Chicago
Also Boston : Atlanta : Dallas
San Francisco : Portland

ACKNOWLEDGMENT

The verses on pages 9, 25, 41, and 45 are from *Choral Speaking Arrangements for the Lower Grades,* by Louise Abney, copyright 1937 by the Expression Company, and are used by special arrangement.

AM : TWBS-4

Copyright 1940 by World Book Company
Copyright in Great Britain
All rights reserved

PRINTED IN U.S.A.

GUIDES TO BETTER SPEECH

As you travel on the road to Better Speech, you will be talking. Why not talk well? Here are some guides to Better Speech.

1. Do I stand straight when I speak?
2. Do I sit straight while I listen?
3. Do I wait until everyone is ready to listen to me?
4. Do I use a friendly voice?
5. Do I speak so that everyone can hear me?
6. Do I speak too fast?
7. Do I speak too slowly?
8. Do I speak plainly?

Can you think of other guides to Better Speech? Add them to this list.

• •

On the road to Better Speech, you will need to use your LIPS, TONGUE, JAWS, and PALATE. These are your speech helpers.

Here are some exercises that will guide you to Better Speech. Practice them every day. Practicing before a mirror will help.

LIP EXERCISES

Make these sounds:

> *ee-oo, ee-oo, ee-oo*
> *wee-woo, wee-woo, wee-woo*
> *me, me, me, me, mo*

TONGUE EXERCISES

Make your tongue touch your nose: *Up-in, up-in, up-in.* Make your tongue touch your chin: *Down-in, down-in, down-in.* Swing your tongue left and right: *Left-right, left-right, left-right.*

Make your tongue go around the outside of your mouth. With your tongue pointed, dot the roof of your mouth in three places: *Front, middle, back.* Groove your tongue.

Sweep the roof of your mouth with the point of your tongue: *Front to back, back to front.*

EXERCISES FOR YOUR JAWS

Make these sounds:

ah-oo, ah-oo, ah-oo

hee-haw, hee-haw, hee-haw

USING YOUR PALATE

Your palate has two parts.

The front of the roof of your mouth is your hard palate. The hard palate does not move. Tap your tongue to sound the letter T. You are now tapping your hard palate.

The back of the roof of your mouth is your soft palate. It can move. Say *ung-ah, ung-ah*. Do you feel your soft palate move?

Exercise your soft palate by saying:

ung-ah, ung-ah, ung-ah

ing-ick, ing-ick, ing-ick

ding-dong, ding-dong, ding-dong

• •

In speaking, you must move your lips, tongue, jaws, and palate. This is the first step along the way to Better Speech.

SOUNDS AND SOUND COUSINS

Along the way to Better Speech we shall meet old friends. These friends are sounds.

There are many kinds of sounds. Some are made with your lips, as M. Some are made with your lips and teeth, as F. Some are made with your tongue and teeth, as TH. Some are made with your tongue and palate, as L.

You will meet all these sounds on the way to Better Speech.

• •

Some sounds have cousins just as you do.

Sound cousins are made alike, but they have different voices. One has a deep voice. One whispers. You can feel the sounds with deep voices in your throat.

Put your hand lightly across your throat and sound B. Now sound P.

These two sounds are cousins. P whispers; B talks with a deep voice.

Sounds that whisper like P are called *breath sounds*.

Sounds with deep voices like B are called *voiced sounds*.

You can always feel the voiced sounds in your throat.

F and V are cousins. Sound them.
Which one whispers?
Which one has a deep voice?
Look for other cousins along the way to Better Speech.

I am the M sound.
I am made with two lips.
I am made with breath.
I hum when I talk.
Make me hum.
Can you feel me
 in your nose?

Sounds you can feel in your nose are called *nasal* sounds.

• •

Here are some words I begin.   Pronounce them aloud.

me	man	more	mother
my	mail	moon	Mary
may	meat	many	Monday

Can you think of other words I begin?   Write them. Now pronounce them.

• •

Here are some words I end.   Pronounce them aloud.

| hum | home | drum | dream |
| come | seem | came | them |

Can you think of other words I end?   Write them. Now pronounce them.

Read these sentences aloud:

1. My mother misses me.
2. Martha made mud pies on Monday.
3. Mother makes me drink milk at home.
4. Mary made May baskets on May Day.
5. I had a dream and it didn't seem real.
6. The mailman made many trips.

Make other sentences using the M sound. Read them aloud.

• •

Here is a poem for you. Make the M's hum!

MY TOP AND I

My top is humming a happy song.
It hums and hums the whole day long:
   M-m-m, M-m-m, M-m-m.

It dances in a merry ring;
Its music makes me want to sing:
   M-m-m, M-m-m, M-m-m.

I like the merry humming song
It's spinning as it moves along:
   M-m-m, M-m-m, M-m-m.

Now it's stopped; its humming done.
My top and I have lots of fun!
   M-m-m, M-m-m, M-m-m.

I am the P sound.
I am made with two lips.
I am made with breath.
I send little puffs of breath between the lips.
Put your hand in front of your lips and sound me.
Can you feel the little puffs?

• •

Here are some words I begin. Pronounce them aloud.

pop	pipe	park	pepper
pan	papa	paper	puppet
pet	pass	puppy	pumpkin

Can you think of other words I begin? Write them. Now pronounce them.

• •

Here are some words I end. Pronounce them aloud.

| top | step | bump | pup |
| mop | flop | pump | stop |

Can you think of other words I end? Write them. Now pronounce them.

[8]

Read these sentences aloud:

1. "Pup — pup — pup," puffed the motor boat.
2. Please pass the pumpkin pie.
3. Paul played ping-pong.
4. Poor pussy put her paw in the puddle.
5. The puppy pulled at a piece of paper.
6. We had a picnic by the pond in the park.

Make other sentences using the P sound. Read them aloud.

• •

Here is a poem for you. Make the pop-corn "pop."

THE SONG OF THE POP-CORN

"Pop — pop — pop!"
Says the pop-corn in the pan;
"Pop — pop — pop!
You may catch me if you can!"

"Pop — pop — pop!"
Says each kernel, hard and yellow:
"Pop — pop — pop!
I'm a dancing little fellow!"

"Pop — pop — pop!
I can whirl and skip and hop!"
Pop — pop — pop — pop!
  Pop! Pop! POP!

I am the B sound.
To make me use two lips.
Make your breath go
 through your lips.
Sound me in your throat.
Put your hand across your
 throat.

Can you feel me as I talk? I am a cousin of the P sound. Do you know why?

• •

Here are some words I begin. Pronounce them aloud.

be	boy	bone	bounce
bus	baby	barn	bush
bat	ball	boat	boot

Can you think of other words I begin? Write them. Now pronounce them.

• •

Here are some words I end. Pronounce them aloud.

| cob | cub | job | web |
| Bob | cab | bib | tub |

Can you think of other words I end? Write them. Now pronounce them.

Read these sentences aloud:

1. "Buzz," said the Bumble Bee, "buzz, buzz."
2. Bob bounced the ball to the boys.
3. The baby has a bib.
4. Big black bunnies like beets.
5. Brownies wear bright bells on their boots.
6. "Bow-wow," barked Bowser, the bulldog.

Make other sentences using the B sound. Read them aloud.

• •

This poem will give you practice on the B sounds. Open your jaws wide as you say "baa."

NIBBLE NOSE

Nibble Nose is our pet goat,
    Baa, baa, baa;
He wears a soft and silky coat,
    Baa, baa, baa.

He gets his lunch by nibbling grass,
    Baa, baa, baa;
And greets the children as they pass,
    Baa, baa, baa.

Day by day, he grows and grows,
    Baa, baa, baa;
He'll soon grow up, our Nibble Nose,
    Baa, baa, baa.

I am the W sound.
I am made with lips.
I am made with voice.
Make your lips round and say "oo" like the wind.
That's how I sound.

• •

Here are some words I begin. Pronounce them aloud.

was   work   walk   woman
wash   will   wish   wiggle
well   wood   water   wagon

Can you think of other words I begin? Write them. Now pronounce them.

• •

Read these sentences aloud.

1. Wee Willie Winkie waked early on Wednesday.
2. He went wading.
3. Polliwogs wiggled in the water.
4. The windmill waved its arms as the wind blew.

5. A woodpecker will peck wood.
6. I wish I had a wagon with little wire wheels.

Make other sentences using the W sound. Read them aloud.

• •

Read this story aloud.

A WEE TALE OF A WEE WOMAN

A wee wee woman lived in a wee wee house.
The wee wee house had a wee wee window.
One day the wee wee woman went away.
She went on her wee wee way by her wee wee self.
People wondered where the wee wee woman was.
For weeks and weeks they wondered where she was.
They believed that the witches had whisked her away.
What would you think of that?
Where would you think the wee wee woman was?
We will wonder always.
The wind knows, but he won't tell where.
"Oo — oo," wails the wind, "Oo — oo!"
I know! I know! Do you?

I am the WH sound.
I am made with lips.
I am made with breath.
Now turn me around and sound H-W.
That's how I am made.

• •

Here are some words I begin. Pronounce them aloud.

why	whale	white	which
when	wheat	while	whittle
wheel	where	whirl	whistle

Can you think of other words I begin? Write them. Now pronounce them.

• •

Read these sentences aloud:

1. The wheel said, "Whir, whir, whir."
2. Where is my white whistle?
3. Why do Eskimos want to kill whales?
4. I will wheel the wheelbarrow wherever you wish.

5. In which tree was the whippoorwill?
6. The wheat waved when the wind blew.

Make other sentences using the WH sound. Read them aloud.

• •

Hold a sheet of thin paper before your mouth. Sound W, then WH. What happens?

• •

Practice these words, going down the lists. Then practice these words, going across the lists.

W	WH
way	whey
witch	which
wear	where
wail	whale
weather	whether
world	whirled
were	whir

Can you *hear* the difference as you pronounce them? Can you *feel* the difference?

I am the F sound.
I am made with lower lip.
I am made with the upper teeth.
Scratch your lower lip lightly against your upper teeth.
Now blow lightly at the same time.

• •

Here are some words I begin. Pronounce them aloud.

fan	face	fool	fairy
fun	find	farm	father
fix	fish	field	Friday

Can you think of other words I begin? Write them. Now pronounce them.

• •

Here are some words I end. Pronounce them aloud.

| muff | huff | calf | loaf |
| puff | stuff | half | roof |

Can you think of other words I end? Write them. Now pronounce them.

Read these sentences aloud:

1. Father fished on Friday.
2. Firemen fought the fire.
3. Frank had fun with the calf.
4. We have fresh fruit for breakfast.
5. The fairy found a flower muff.
6. Running makes me puff and puff.

Make other sentences using the F sound. Read them aloud.

• •

Practice on the F sound. Read these aloud.

KITTY

Fa, fe, fi, fo, fu,
Kitty says "Mew, mew,
I shall follow after you."
Fa, fe, fi, fo, fu.

FAIRIES

Fairies are my friends.
Once I found one in my front yard.
He was a funny little fellow.
He frowned when I found him.

I am the V sound.
I am made with lower lip.
I am made with the upper teeth.
Scratch your lower lip lightly against your upper teeth.
Now use your voice.
Whose cousin am I? How are we alike? How are we not alike?

• •

Here are some words I begin. Pronounce them aloud.

van   vote   visit   vine   violets
very   valley vase   voice   valentine

Can you think of other words I begin? Write them. Now pronounce them.

• •

Here are some words I end. Pronounce them aloud.

give   five   have   live   love

Can you think of other words I end? Write them. Now pronounce them.

Read these sentences aloud:

1. "V-v-v-v-v-v-v," hums the airplane.
2. Have you a very soft voice?
3. Vera found a valentine.
4. The valentine said, "I love you."
5. Puppies are very lively.
6. We found violets in the valley.

Make other sentences using the V sound. Read them aloud.

• •

Sometimes B is sounded when V should be sounded. Do you know the difference? Here are some words beginning with the two sounds. Practice these words going down the lists. Then practice these words going across the lists.

B	V
berry	very
ban	van
best	vest
base	vase
bow	vow
boat	vote

I am the TH sound.
I am made with the tongue.
I am made with the teeth.
I am made with breath.
Put the tip of your tongue between your teeth and blow.

• •

Here are some words I begin.   Pronounce them aloud.

thin	think	thumb	throw
thaw	thank	thimble	throat
thick	thirty	thistle	thrush

Can you think of other words I begin? Write them. Now pronounce them.

• •

Here are some words I end.   Pronounce them aloud.

| teeth | forth | worth | birth |
| south | north | mouth | earth |

Can you think of other words I end? Write them. Now pronounce them.

[20]

Read these sentences aloud:
1. Think before you talk.
2. Thanksgiving is a day of thanks.
3. Always say, "Thank you."
4. The thick ice began to thaw.
5. Throw the thistle away.
6. The nurse looked at my mouth, my teeth, and my throat.

Make other sentences using the TH sound. Read them aloud.

• •

Read this poem aloud.

A CHILD'S GRACE

Thank you for the world so sweet,
Thank you for the food we eat,
Thank you for the birds that sing,
Thank you, God, for everything.

An English Grace

I am another TH sound.
I am also made with voice.
Sound me by saying the word *this*.
Now say *thin*.
Can you feel the difference?

• •

Here are some words I begin. Pronounce them aloud.

| they | them | these | this |
| that | there | those | their |

Can you think of other words I begin? Write them. Now pronounce them.

• •

I am in the middle of these words. Pronounce them aloud.

| mother | father | weather | gather |
| other | brother | bother | either |

Can you think of other words? Write them. Now pronounce them.

Read these sentences aloud:

1. There they are.
2. Their father and mother will go.
3. They will take their brother with them.
4. They like this weather.
5. Do you want these or those?
6. Do not bother mother.

Make other sentences using the TH sound. Read them aloud.

I am the T sound.
I am made with the tongue.
I am made with breath.
Tap your tongue back of your upper teeth.
That's how I am made.

• •

Here are some words I begin. Pronounce them aloud.

toe	toy	tool	tiny
tan	tell	time	took
top	tea	tear	table

Can you think of other words I begin? Write them. Now pronounce them.

• •

Here are some words I end. Pronounce them aloud.

| it | hot | get | meat |
| let | sat | just | boat |

Can you think of other words I end? Write them. Now pronounce them.

Read these sentences aloud:
1. Tip, tap, tap your tongue.
   Tip, tap, the T's will come.
2. "Tick-tock, tick-tock," ticked the clock.
3. Take the hot tea to the table.
4. Let me get my top.
5. Tom just took a toy boat to Teddy.
6. Tap, tap, came the tapping of the rain.

Make other sentences using the T sound.

• •

The clock says "Tick-tock." Play you are the clock.

THE NURSERY CLOCK

The nursery clock hangs high on the wall,
   Tick-tock, tick-tock;
And every morning I hear its voice call —
   Tick, tick, tock!

High on the wall it is running all day,
   Tick-tock, tick-tock;
Ticking the minutes and seconds away —
   Tick, tick, tock!

Each morning it hustles me out of my bed,
   Tick-tock, tick-tock;
At evening it's ticking while prayers are said —
   Tick, tick, tock!

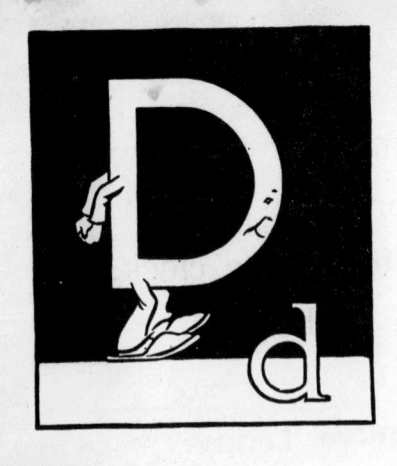

I am the D sound.
I am made with the tongue.
Tap your tongue back of your upper teeth.
Now use your voice on this sound.

Whose cousin am I? How are we alike? How are we not alike?

• •

Here are some words I begin. Pronounce them aloud.

do	day	deep	ditch
dot	dog	duck	dance
den	doll	dirty	dress

Can you think of other words I begin? Write them. Now pronounce them.

• •

Here are some words I end. Pronounce them aloud.

| did | mud | David | good |
| dad | seed | blood | food |

Can you think of other words I end? Write them. Now pronounce them.

Read these sentences aloud:

1. Donald Duck was dirty.
2. Dot dressed her doll.
3. Dad dug a deep, deep ditch.
4. David ate doughnuts for dinner.
5. Drive down through town.
6. The dog played in the mud.

Make other sentences using the D sound. Read them aloud.

Look for the D's in this poem.

THE GRAY BILLY-GOAT

Grandmother had a little gray billy-goat,
Dinkums, dunkums, little gray billy-goat.
Granny was fond of her little gray billy-goat,
Dinkums, dunkums, little gray billy-goat.

Little gray billy-goat thought he'd go a-walking,
Dinkums, dunkums, little gray billy-goat.
Big gray wolves came stalking, a-stalking.
Dinkums, dunkums, little gray billy-goat.

All that was found was his hoofs and his horns,
Dinkums, dunkums, little gray billy-goat.
Grandmother sits by the stove and mourns,
Dinkums, dunkums, little gray billy-goat.

Russian Folk Song

I am the S sound.
I am made with the tongue.
I am made with breath.
Put your teeth together.
Now blow or hiss.

Be sure to hide your tongue behind your teeth.

• •

Here are some words I begin. Pronounce them aloud.

so	saw	sail	seat
see	sing	song	soup
say	soon	soap	salt

Can you think of other words I begin? Write them. Now pronounce them.

• •

Here are some words I end. Pronounce them aloud.

| sits | speaks | slips | miss |
| steps | stops | sleeps | pass |

Can you think of other words I end? Write them. Now pronounce them.

In some words I am written C instead of S. Pronounce these words.

ice   fence   place   face   sauce   space

Can you think of other words? Write them. Now pronounce them.

• •

Read these sentences aloud:

1. Sing a song of sixpence.
2. Sally slipped on the ice.
3. My sister put salt in the soup.
4. We saw ice on the steps.
5. Always practice safety.
6. See the stars and stripes.

Make other sentences using the S sound. Read them aloud.

• •

Practice this verse aloud.

> The snowflakes are falling
> By ones and by twos.
> There is snow on my jacket
> And snow on my shoes;
> There is snow on the bushes
> And snow on the trees,
> It's snowing on everything
> Now, if you please.

I am the Z sound.
I am made with the tongue.
I am made with breath.
Put your teeth together.
Now blow and use your voice.
Hide your tongue behind your teeth.
Whose cousin am I? How are we alike?
How are we not alike?

• •

Here are some words I begin. Pronounce them aloud.

zoo   zero   zig-zag   zebra   zoom   zone

• •

I am in the middle of these words. Pronounce them.

busy   cozy   daisy   visit   lazy   cousin

• •

Here are some words I end. Pronounce them.

is   nose   days   buzz   bees   cars

Can you think of other words in which I am found? Write them. Now pronounce them.

Read these sentences aloud:

1. "Zzz, zzz, zzz," buzzed the bees.
2. My cousin is busy.
3. There is a zebra in the zoo.
4. We visit the zoo on Saturdays.
5. The cars go zig-zag.
6. Please sell me some daisies.

Make and read other sentences using the Z sound.

• •

Make the airplane "zoom."

THE AIRPLANE

Zoom, zoom, zoom,
   Hear the airplanes hum!
Zoom, zoom, zoom,
   See how fast they come.

Make the bee "buzz."

THE SONG OF THE BEE

The bee is singing a song,
   Zzz, zzz, zzz,
To each flower as he flits along —
   Zzz, zzz, zzz.
While father makes money,
The bee makes his honey
In hours that are sunny —
   Zzz, zzz, zzz.

I am the SH sound.
I am made with the lips.
I am made with the tongue.
I am made with breath.

Push your lips forward, lift your tongue a little, then blow.

• •

Here are some words I begin. Pronounce them aloud.

shoe   shells   show   shear
shop   sheep   sheet   shower
ship   shine   shore   should

• •

Here are some words I end. Pronounce them aloud.

dish   bush   rush   fish   mush   sash

Can you think of other words I begin or end? Write them. Now pronounce them.

• •

Who is my cousin? This will help you. Who is the cousin of S? Now add an H. Now voice the sound.

Here are words with the ZH sound (voiced SH):

        pleasure   treasure

Can you think of others?

• •

Read these sentences aloud:

1. She sells sea shells on the sea shore.
2. Let's have a show in the shack.
3. He should shear the sheep.
4. Put the fish in the dish.
5. There was a treasure on the ship.
6. The sun will shine after the shower.

Make other sentences using the SH sound. Read them aloud.

• •

Read this poem aloud for practice.

A LULLABY

Hush-a-by, hush-a-by,
Go to sleep, dear.
Hush-a-by, hush-a-by,
Mother is here.

She will not leave you,
She will be near,
Hush-a-by, hush-a-by,
Go to sleep, dear!

I am the CH sound.
I am made with two sounds.
I am made with breath.
Sound T and SH close together and that makes me, CH.

Sound them close together, T-SH.

• •

Here are some words I begin.   Pronounce them aloud.

child	chew	chirp	children
chop	churn	chief	chicken
chair	chose	cheese	chimney

Can you think of other words I begin?   Write them. Now pronounce them.

• •

Here are some words I end.   Pronounce them aloud.

| such | reach | peach | patch |
| much | lunch | church | perch |

Can you think of other words I end?   Write them. Now pronounce them.

[34]

Read these sentences aloud:

1. " Cheep-cheep," chirped the chicken, " cheep-cheep."
2. " Chug, chug, chug," chugged the motor boat.
3. Can the child reach the peach?
4. Charles ate cheese for lunch.
5. The children chose the chairs for the church.
6. We chose the chief.

Make other sentences using the CH sound. Read them aloud.

This poem is good practice for the CH sound.

THE TRAIN

"T-sh, t-sh, choo, choo, choo,"
Said the chugging little train.
"T-sh, t-sh, choo, choo, choo
I am chugging in the rain."

[35]

I am the J sound.
I am made with two sounds.
I am made with voice.
D and ZH make J.
Whose cousin am I?

Sound D and ZH close together and that makes me, J.

Here are some words I begin. Pronounce them aloud.

jam	joy	jelly	judge
jaw	just	jolly	June
jar	joke	jump	jockey

Can you think of other words I begin? Write them. Now pronounce them.

Read these sentences aloud.

1. "Jay, jay," says the blue jay.
2. Jean jumped the jumping rope.
3. Joe and John joined the Junior Red Cross in June.

[36]

4. Jane got the jam and the jelly.
5. I have a giant jumping jack.
6. Jack was a jockey.

Make other sentences using the J sound. Read them aloud.

• •

Read these aloud.

"Jay . . . jay" . . . from far away
Came the call of the bright blue jay.

JINGLE BELLS

Jingle bells,
Jingle bells,
Jingle all the way!
Oh what fun
It is to ride
In a one-horse open sleigh!
Jingle bells,
Jingle bells,
Jingle all the way!

JOLLY JUMPING JACK

I am a jolly Jumping Jack
In a box of red and black.
Lift the lid and I jump out.
See me smile? I never pout.

I am the L sound.
I am made with the tongue.
I am made with voice.
Press the tip of your tongue against your hard palate.

The sound comes out at the sides of your tongue.

• •

Here are some words I begin.   Pronounce them aloud.

lay	left	lamp	ladies
lot	long	lamb	lollipop
lost	lick	light	lullaby

Can you think of other words I begin?   Write them. Now pronounce them.

• •

Here are some words I end.   Pronounce them aloud.

pal	fall	fool	pull
ball	dull	mule	roll

Can you think of other words I end?   Write them. Now pronounce them.

[38]

Read these sentences aloud:

1. "Lu, lu, lu," is a lullaby.
2. Lee lost his little ball when he fell.
3. I like to lick lollipops.
4. Little ladies like lemonade.
5. Come along; let's play leapfrog.
6. I saw the mule fall.

Make other sentences using the L sound. Read them aloud.

• •

"Lumpety, lumpety, lump" is fun to say. Find these words in this poem. Say them.

A FARMER WENT RIDING

A farmer went trotting upon his gray mare,
  Bumpety, bumpety, bump!
With his daughter behind him so rosy and fair,
  Lumpety, lumpety, lump!
A raven cried "croak!" and they all tumbled down,
  Bumpety, bumpety, bump!
The mare broke her knees and the farmer his crown,
  Lumpety, lumpety, lump!
The mischievous raven flew laughing away,
  Bumpety, bumpety, bump!
And vowed he would serve them the same the next day.
  Lumpety, lumpety, lump!

Old Folk Rhyme

I am the R sound.
I am made with the tongue.
I am made with voice.
Lift the tip of your tongue a little and then curl it back.
Now sound me, R.

• •

Here are some words I begin.   Pronounce them aloud.

rod	ready	roof	radio
row	rope	rain	rock
read	road	room	Rover

Can you think of other words I begin?   Write them. Now pronounce them.

• •

Here are some words I end.   Pronounce them aloud.

| cover | mother | four | sister |
| river | father | sour | summer |

Can you think of other words I end?   Write them. Now pronounce them.

[40]

Read these sentences aloud:

1. Be ready to read.
2. "Erp, erp," barked the little dog.
3. A rabbit ran around the rock.
4. A robin redbreast was in the rain.
5. Run to the river with Rover.
6. Father rows our boat in the summer.

Make other sentences using the R sound. Read them aloud.

• •

Read aloud. Make your rap-a-taps sound like the rain.

SUMMER RAIN

Rap-a-tap-tap
Comes the summer rain;
Rap-a-tap-tap
On the window pane.

Rap-a-tap-tap
It is waking the flowers;
Rap-a-tap-tap
Come the summer showers.

Rap-a-tap-tap
It sings to the grass;
Rap-a-tap-tap,
The raindrops pass.

I am the N sound.
I am made with the tongue.
Press your tongue against your hard palate.
Now sound me in your nose.

Do you remember that the sounds you send through your nose are called *nasal* sounds?

• •

Here are some words I begin. Pronounce them aloud.

no	noon	nice	name
nod	new	nail	nurse
nose	nap	need	nursery

Can you think of other words I begin? Write them. Now pronounce them.

• •

Here are some words I end. Pronounce them aloud.

| pan | fun | tin | ten |
| ran | sun | nine | tan |

Can you think of other words I end? Write them. Now pronounce them.

Read these sentences aloud:
1. "Neigh, neigh, neigh," said the horse.
2. We need ten new needles.
3. Ned had fun in the sun.
4. Nan went to the nursery to take a nap.
5. The new nurse is in the nursery.
6. By noon I must know nine new names.

Make other sentences using the N sound. Read them aloud.

• •

How many N's can you find in this poem? (Be sure to find the N sounds in the middle of the words and at the end, too.) Read it aloud.

NANNY IS MY NURSE

Nanny is my nurse's name,
   She's very, very good,
If I behave the best I can,
   As all nice children should.

Nanny is the nicest nurse.
   She's never, never cross
Except when *I* am naughty —
   Then Nanny shows who's boss.

I am the NG sound.

I am made with the tongue.

I am made with the soft palate.

Make the back of your tongue touch your soft palate.

Now sound me in your nose.

Remember that my two letters NG make *one* sound.

M, N, and NG are the three nasal sounds.

• •

There are many words I end. Here are some of them. Pronounce them aloud.

bang	bring	ping-pong
sang	swing	dingdong
rang	song	walking
sing	ringing	talking
wing	getting	sliding

Can you think of other words I end? Write them. Now pronounce them.

Read these sentences aloud:

1. "Dingdong," the bells are ringing.
2. "Ting-a-ling," the telephone jingled.
3. She sang a song.
4. I like to sing and swing.
5. Bring the ping-pong balls.
6. I am getting a singing bird.

Make other sentences using the NG sound. Read them aloud.

• •

This poem gives practice on the –ING endings. Read it aloud.

SNOWFLAKES

Feathery flakes of snow come down,
   Swirling, twirling, drifting,
Until they cover all the town,
   Swirling, twirling, drifting.
People hurry to and fro,
   Riding, sliding, skipping,
Through the silver-powdered snow,
   Riding, sliding, skipping.
Motor cars are going home,
   Shifting, swerving, dripping —
Through the swirling snowy-foam
   Shifting, swerving, dripping.

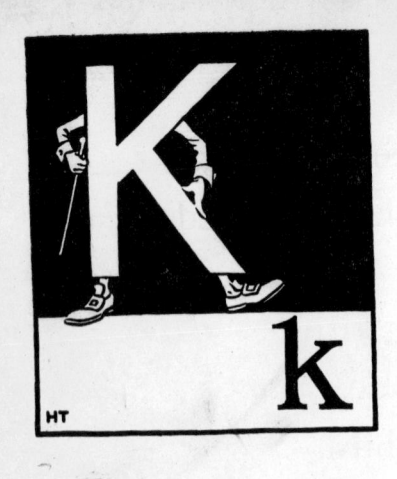

I am the K sound.
I am made with the tongue.
I am made with the soft palate.
I am made with breath.

Tap the back of your tongue against your soft palate.

Now send your breath out.

In some words I am written C instead of K.

Here are some words I begin. Pronounce them aloud.

    car   cat   candy   crow
    cap   cut   catch   come
    key   kite   count   kangaroo

Here are some words I end. Pronounce them aloud.

cake   take   kick   look   book   make

Can you think of other words I begin or end? Write them. Now pronounce them.

Read these sentences aloud:

1. " Caw, caw," called the crow.
2. Ask Carl to cut the cake.
3. Catch my kite quickly.
4. The cat carried the cute kitten.
5. Come and count your candy eggs.
6. Take a look at the book.

Make other sentences using the K sound. Read them aloud.

• •

Read aloud for practice.

GETTING-UP TIME

"Bow-wow," said the pup,
"It is time to get up."

"Coo-coo," said the dove,
From the roof high above.

"Moo-moo," said the cow,
"I am getting up now."

"Caw, caw," called the crow,
"What makes you so slow?"

I am the G sound.
I am made with the tongue.
I am made with the soft palate.
Tap the back of your tongue against your soft palate. Now use your voice.

Whose cousin am I? How are we alike? How are we not alike?

• •

Here are some words I begin. Pronounce them aloud.

    go   girl   gobble   glasses
    get   gave   green   grandma
    gate   game   ground   glad

Can you think of other words I begin? Write them. Now pronounce them

• •

Here are some words I end. Pronounce them aloud.

    big   dig   pig   jig   wig   dog

Can you think of other words I end? Write them. Now pronounce them.

Read these sentences aloud:

1. " Gobble, gobble, gobble," said the turkey.
2. " Gr-r-r," growled the grizzly bear.
3. Get grandma's glasses for her.
4. Green grass grows on the ground.
5. Girls and boys are glad to play games.
6. I saw the dog dig.

Make other sentences using the G sound. Read them aloud.

• •

Watch the G endings in this poem.

THE LAZY PIG

A little fat pig
In a big white wig
Was busily dancing
A jig, jig, jig.
"Wee, wee," said the pig
In the big white wig.
"I'd much rather jig
Than dig, dig, dig."

I am the QU sound.
I am made with two sounds.
I am made with K and W.
Sound K and W close together.
That makes me, QU.

• •

Here are some words I begin.   Pronounce them aloud.

queer   quack   quart   quickly
quilt   quite   quarter quietly
quiet   quick   queen   quarrel

Can you think of other words I begin?   Write them. Now pronounce them.

• •

Read these sentences aloud:

1. "Quack, quack," quacked the duck.
2. The queen came quickly.
3. "Be quiet," said the Queen.
4. Two quarts of milk will cost a quarter.

5. The quilt was quite pretty.
6. We slipped quietly away.

Make other sentences using the QU sound. Read them aloud.

• •

Can you sound the many QU's in these poems?

TWO LITTLE GIRLS

Quaint and Queer are two little girls,
   With quiet ways and golden curls;
Quaint likes quilting, Queer likes books;
   Both enjoy quiet nooks.

SQUEAKY MOUSE

Squeak! Squeak! Squeak! Squeak!
What's all this clatter I hear?
Squeaky Mouse has caught his tail
In a trap, I fear.

SAMMY SQUIRREL

"Why are you cross, Sammy Squirrel?"
Questioned his mother one day.
"You quite forgot your manners
When Squeaky Mouse came to play."

I am the H sound.

I am made with open lips.

I am made with a little puff of breath.

I am made as quietly as breathing.

Send a little puff of breath through your open lips.

• •

Here are some words I begin. Pronounce them aloud.

hop	hear	high	hope
hall	home	hard	head
hang	hold	horse	hoop

Can you think of other words I begin? Write them. Now pronounce them.

• •

Read these sentences aloud:

1. "Hoo, hoo," hooted the hoot owl.
2. Hop, hop, hop, all the way home.
3. Hold your head high.
4. Hans and Hilda live in Holland.

5. Hang your hats in the hall.
6. Helen played with the hoop and hummed.

Make other sentences using the H sound. Read them aloud.

• •

This poem gives practice on the H's.

HIPPETY HIPPETY HOP

A little white bunny
Went out to play —
   Hippety, hippety, hop;
A little black bunny
Came down the way —
   Hippety, hippety, hop.

The two little bunnies
Had fun that day —
   Hippety, hippety, hop;
They spoke to each other
In the very best way —
   Hippety, hippety, hop.

The little black bunny
Then turned to say —
   (Hippety, hippety, hop)
"I'd like to play, but I cannot stay.
Let's meet again some other day —"
   Hippety, hippety, hop!

I am the Y sound.
Sometimes I sound almost
  like the E in *me*.
Can you hear my voice
  as you say *yes*?
I am made with voice.

• •

Here are some words I begin.   Pronounce them aloud.

yes	yell	yellow	yeast
you	yard	youth	yesterday
yet	year	young	yardstick

Can you think of other words I begin?   Write them. Now pronounce them.

• •

Read these sentences aloud:

1. " Yoo-oo-oo, yoo-oo-oo," moans the wind.
2. Yellow flowers are in the yard.
3. You may play in the yard.
4. The yolk was yellow.
5. Is your young brother with you?
6. Yes, I have a yellow yardstick.

Make other sentences using the Y sound. Read them aloud.

• •

Hans is from Holland. It's fun to talk as he does.

THE BOY NEXT DOOR

Hans has come across the sea
To live next door and play with me.
Hans says "Yah" when I say "Yes,"
But he knows what I mean, I guess.
    Yah, yah, yah . . .
    Yes, yes, yes . . .
Hans knows what I mean, I guess.

I am the X sound.
I am made with two sounds.
Do you know what they are?
I am made with breath.
K and S make X.

• •

Here are some words I end. Pronounce them aloud.

ax	fox	tax	annex
ox	wax	fix	coax
box	mix	six	relax

Can you think of other words I end? Write them. Now pronounce them.

• •

The endings of these words sound the same as I do but are written KS.

asks	locks	works	talks
socks	rocks	ticks	tacks
picks	knocks	kicks	sticks

Can you think of other words? Write them. Now pronounce them.

Read these sentences aloud:

1. The fox is in the box.
2. She works on books.
3. A wax candle is in the box.
4. Mother bakes as the clock ticks.
5. She asks us to use the walks.
6. Do not mix the socks.

Make other sentences using the X sound. Read them aloud.

Our name is A.
There are five of us.
We are quintuplets.
Each of us will speak to you.
Each of us has a different sound.

ā

I am the Long A sound.
Spread the corners of your lips.
Now lift your tongue and
   say *ate*.
I begin that word.
I have a line above me.
I look like this: ā

• •

I am in these words. Pronounce them aloud.

may	say	ate	play
pay	jay	mate	plate
way	lay	wait	place
day	hay	gate	take

Write and pronounce other words using Long A.

• •

Can you find the Long A's in these sentences? Read them aloud.

1. They play all day in the hay.
2. May I wait at the gate?
3. Amos and Andy are on the radio.
4. Say "thank you" when you take the plate.

Make and read aloud other sentences using Long A.

ă

I am the Short A sound.
Lift your tongue a little.
Widen your jaws.
I begin the word *at*.
I have a curve above me.
I look like this: ă

• •

I am in these words. Pronounce them aloud.

at	fat	am	bad
mat	cat	man	sad
pat	sat	pan	lad
bat	hat	can	glad

Can you think of other words using Short A? Write them. Now pronounce them.

• •

Read these sentences aloud.

1. A little cat sat on a mat.
2. The fat man wore a hat.
3. An apple pie is in the pan.
4. I am glad I can bat the ball.

Can you make other sentences? Read them aloud.

ä

I am A with One Dot above me.
Your teeth and lips are not so wide apart as for Short A.
Your tongue is held lower.
My voice is softer than Short A's.

I look like this: ä

• •

I am in these words. Pronounce them aloud.

ask	fast	glass	pasture
after	last	bath	prance
pass	class	path	chance
past	grass	dance	glance

Can you think of other words with A's like these? Write and pronounce them.

• •

Read these sentences aloud. Make others.

1. Keep off the grass.
2. Let us dance along the path.
3. Ask him to pass the glass.
4. The last one in the class may pass.

Can you make other sentences? Read them aloud.

ä I am A with Two Dots above me.
Open your mouth wide.
Now say *ah*.
Your jaws are far apart when I talk.

I look like this: ä

• •

I am in these words. Pronounce them aloud.

are	star	farm	mamma
far	arm	mark	papa
tar	barn	park	father
car	harm	bark	aunt

Can you think of other words with A's like these? Write and pronounce them.

• •

Read these sentences aloud.

1. We are going to the park.
2. Mamma and papa are going in the car.
3. The star is far, far away.
4. There are animals in the barn on the farm.

Make other sentences. Read them aloud.

ą

I am A with Two Dots under me.
Your lips are round when
   I talk.
I begin the word *all*.
I have a very deep voice.
I look like this : ą

• •

I am in these words.   Pronounce them aloud.

paw	all	walk	dawn
saw	ball	talk	salt
caw	fall	caught	water
draw	tall	chalk	daughter

Can you think of other words with A's like these? Write them and pronounce them.

• •

Read these sentences aloud.

1. Stand tall when you talk.
2. I saw the ball fall.
3. There was water on the walk.
4. " Caw, caw," said the crow, " caw, caw."

Can you make other sentences?   Read them aloud.

Here are other sentences. All members of the A family are in them. Read them aloud. Can you hear the voice of each one?

Long A   ā

Short A   ă

A with One Dot above it   ȧ

A with Two Dots above it   ä

A with Two Dots under it   ạ

Remember, each has a different sound.

1. They play all day in the alley.
2. Take a nap in father's lap.
3. My aunt made an apple pie.
4. Ask your daddy if I may wait in his car.
5. The cat placed her paws on the paper.
6. A small package lay on the table.
7. We shall have a dancing party this afternoon.
8. Can you draw pictures of a gate, a barn, a hat, a glass, and a plate?

Our name is E.
There are three of us.
We are triplets.
Each of us will speak to you.
Each of us has a different sound.

ē

I am the Long E sound.
Spread your lips.
Keep your teeth slightly apart.
I begin the word *eat*.
I have a line above me.
I look like this: ē

• •

I am in these words. Pronounce them aloud.

eat	ear	peep	bead
meat	dear	leap	need
beet	hear	sheep	seed
feet	near	seem	read

Write other words using Long E. Pronounce them aloud.

• •

I am in these sentences. Read them aloud.

1. Did you hear me, dear?
2. Little Bo-Peep has lost her sheep.
3. Come here and play leapfrog.
4. Bunnies eat beets.

Make and read aloud other sentences.

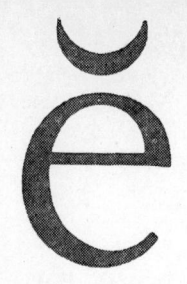

ĕ I am the Short E sound.
Your jaws are not so wide as for Short A.
Lift your tongue a little.
I begin the word *ech*o.
I have a curve above me.
I look like this: ĕ

• •

I am in these words. Pronounce them aloud.

met	net	men	egg
pet	set	pen	beg
bet	let	ten	leg
wet	get	hen	red

Write other words using Short E. Pronounce them aloud.

• •

Read these sentences aloud.
1. Put the hen in the pen.
2. Let me get the eggs.
3. I met ten men.
4. My pet will get wet.

Make other sentences using Short E. Read them.

ẽ

I am the Waved E sound.
I am in the word *her*.
The middle of your tongue is lifted.
I have a waved line above me.
I look like this: ẽ

I am in these words. Pronounce them aloud.

earth	germ	term	perch
earn	herd	verse	search
Earl	heard	nerve	certain
fern	learn	serve	serpent

Write other words using Waved E. Pronounce them aloud.

Read these sentences aloud.

1. Search for a fern.
2. Earl learned a verse.
3. I was certain I heard a bird.
4. We heard the serpent hiss.

Make other sentences using Waved E words. Read them aloud.

Here are other sentences. All members of the E family are in them. Read them aloud. Can you hear the voice of each one?

    Long E ē
    Short E ĕ
    Waved E ẽ

Remember, each has a different sound.

1. Earl earned eleven cents.
2. Ten elves danced merrily under the tree.
3. The little red hen went near the pen.
4. Have you learned that *get* rhymes with *met* and *pet*?

THE ENGINE

Engine, engine, tell me, engine —
 Who's your engineer?
Tell me, engine — could I, engine,
 Be your engineer?

ECHO

Echo, Echo, you're an elf,
Echo here and Echo there.
We hear you, Echo, everywhere.

Our name is I.
There are three of us, too.
We are triplets.
Each of us will speak to you.
Each of us has a different sound.

1

I am the Long I sound.
Sound ȧ and ē close together.
Sound the ē very quickly.
That makes me, Long I.
I have a line above me.
I look like this: ī

• •

I am in these words. Pronounce them aloud.

ice	might	kite	fight
mice	bite	right	fly
nice	night	sight	try
rice	light	white	bright

Write and pronounce other words using Long I.

• •

I am in these sentences. Read them aloud.

1. I like ice cream.
2. I will try to fly my white kite.
3. It is not right to fight.
4. I like bright lights at night.

Make other sentences using Long I words. Read them aloud.

ĭ I am the Short I sound.
I sound almost like Long E (ē).
But I am made more quickly
 and lightly.
I have a curve above me.
I look like this: ĭ

I am in these words. Pronounce them aloud.

it	fit	mitten	whittle
imp	sit	kitten	brittle
pit	pick	little	nimble
bit	stick	children	window

Write other words using Short I. Pronounce them aloud.

Read these sentences aloud.

1. The kitten has my mitten.
2. The little imp was nimble.
3. Let the children sit by the window.
4. Pick two sticks to whittle.

Make other sentences using Short I words. Read them aloud.

ĩ I am the Waved I sound.
I am like the Waved E (ē) sound.
We both talk like the final R (er) sound.
I have a waved line above me.
I look like this: ĩ

• •

I am in these words. Pronounce them aloud.

whir	bird	dirt	whirl
fir	birth	dirty	girl
sir	birthday	thirty	twirl
stir	third	shirt	chirp

Write other words using Waved I. Pronounce them aloud.

• •

Read these sentences aloud.

1. "Whir, whir," said the whirling wheels.
2. It is the little girl's third birthday.
3. The little boy wore a dirty shirt.
4. We heard the bird chirp in the fir tree.

Make other sentences using Waved I words. Read them aloud.

Here are other sentences. All members of the I family are in them. Read them aloud. Can you hear the voice of each one?

Long I   ī

Short I   ĭ

Waved I   ĩ

Remember, each has a different sound.

1. I live in a big city.
2. The girl has a kitten and a bird.
3. I like to slide on the ice in the winter.
4. Is the ice in the ice box?
5. Lightning bugs fly at night.
6. We saw the little girl whirl and twirl.

NIGHT LIGHTS

I like night lights —
Lights that glimmer
Through the mist,
Lights of rose
And amethyst,
Lights upon a moving train,
Lights upon a flying plane,
Lights that shimmer through the rain.

Our name is O.
There are two of us.
We are twins.
Each of us will speak to you.
Each of us has a different sound.

Ō I am the Long O sound.
Round your lips.
Now say *oh*. There I am!
Can you feel my breath?
I have a line above me.
I look like this: ō

• •

I am in these words. Pronounce them aloud.

old	hold	oats	blow
bold	cold	boat	snow
told	gold	coat	grow
sold	row	goat	store

Write other words using Long O. Pronounce them aloud.

• •

Read these sentences aloud.

1. We sold our old goat.
2. It is cold, so wear your coat.
3. We watched the wind blow the snow.
4. Row, row, row your boat.

Make and read aloud other sentences using Long O.

Ŏ   I am the Short O sound.
            I sound much like ä.
            Your throat and mouth are open.
            Your tongue is held very low.
            I have a curve above me.

I look like this: ŏ

• •

I am in these words. Pronounce them aloud.

on	mop	pod	lock
box	top	nod	knock
fox	pot	sod	rock
socks	lot	rod	clock

Write other words using Short O. Pronounce them aloud.

• •

Read these sentences aloud.

1. We saw a fox on the rock.
2. Knock, knock! the door is locked.
3. Tick-tock, tick-tock, ticked the clock.
4. I call my rabbits Mopsy and Topsy.

Make and read aloud other sentences using Short O.

Here are more sentences. Both members of the O family are in them. Read them aloud. Can you hear the voice of each one?

Long O   ō

Short O   ŏ

Remember, each has a different sound.

1. The show was in the lot.
2. We saw lots of snow on the rocks.
3. The wind will blow the sailboat.
4. The socks are sold at the store.
5. Take the gold clock from the box.
6. I put the mop on top of the box.
7. There is a lock on the door of the store.
8. The old goat is eating oats.

Our name is Double O (oo).
There are two of us.
Each of us will speak to you.
Each of us has a different sound.

oo

I am the Long Double O sound.
I am in the word *noon*.
Round your lips into a small circle.
Lift the back of your tongue high.
I look like this: o͞o

• •

I am in these words. Pronounce them aloud.

moon	room	food	pool
boom	boot	hoof	cool
noon	root	roof	spoon
soon	shoot	hoot	broom

Write other words using Long Double O (o͞o). Pronounce them aloud.

• •

Read these sentences aloud. Make others.

1. Boom! Boom! boomed the firecrackers.
2. My balloon sailed up toward the moon.
3. The hoot owl was on the roof.
4. Soon I am going wading in the cool pool.

ŏŏ I am the Short Double O sound.
I am in the word *book*.
Your tongue is not so high as for ōō.
Your lips are not so round.
I look like this: ŏŏ

• •

I am in these words. Pronounce them aloud.

book	cook	brook	hood
took	crook	shook	good
look	crooked	foot	wood
nook	hook	wool	stood

Write other words using Short Double O (ŏŏ). Pronounce them aloud.

• •

Read these sentences aloud. Make others.

1. The cook took a look in her book.
2. I stood by the brook with my fishing hook.
3. Look at the crooked path through the wood.
4. Red Riding Hood met a wolf in the wood.

Both members of the Double O (oo) family are in these sentences. Read them aloud. Can you tell them apart by their voices?

Long Double O $\bar{oo}$

Short Double O $\breve{oo}$

Be sure to make your lips very round for Long Double O ($\bar{oo}$).

1. The wolf stood by the brook and shook himself.
2. Look at my new boots.
3. I stood in my room and looked at the moon.
4. The cook has a good spoon.
5. I took a book and read until noon.
6. Soon I shall sweep the room with my broom.

A JINGLE FOR LONG DOUBLE O's

The Man in the Moon
Ran away with the spoon
Saying, "Always remember
That *soon* rhymes with *noon*.
Room rhymes with *boom*,
Root rhymes with *boot*,
Hoof rhymes with *roof*.
They are Long Double O's.
This rhyme is the *proof!*"

Our name is U.
There are three of us.
We are triplets, too.
Each of us will speak to you.
Each of us has a different sound.

ū

I am the Long U sound.
Sound ĭ and o͞o close together and that makes me, Long U.
I sound like the word *you*.
I have a line above me.
I look like this: ū

• •

I am in these words. Pronounce them aloud.

you	due	tune	beauty
your	duty	Tuesday	suit
use	dew	tube	duke
useful	new	tulip	flute

Write and pronounce other words using Long U.

• •

Pronounce as *you* every Long U in these sentences. Read them aloud.

1. I like your new suit.
2. Play a tune on the flute.
3. We saw dew on the tulips.
4. Buy the radio tubes on Tuesday.

Can you make other sentences with Long U? Read them aloud.

ŭ

I am the Short U sound.
I am made in the middle of your mouth.
I begin the word *us*.
I have a curve above me.
I look like this: ŭ

• •

I am in these words. Pronounce them aloud.

up	but	fun	rug
pup	nut	sun	muff
cup	cut	gun	jump
sup	hut	run	thumb

Write and pronounce other words using Short U.

• •

I am in these sentences. Read them aloud. Can you hear me?

1. The little pup jumped up.
2. We had fun running in the sun.
3. Put the nuts in the cup.
4. I found my muff on the rug.

Make other sentences using Short U words. Read them aloud.

û

I am the Caret U sound.
I sound just like ẽ and ĩ.
R always follows me in words.
See my little peak?
It is called a caret.
I look like this: û

• •

I am in these words. Pronounce them aloud.

purr	hurt	urn	hurl
burr	purse	burn	purple
fur	nurse	turn	burden
cur	purpose	curl	curtain

Can you think of other words using Caret U? Pronounce them aloud.

• •

I am in these sentences. Read them aloud.

1. The little kitten was curled into a fur ball.
2. Did the little girl with curls get hurt?
3. The nurse has lost her purse.
4. I heard my kitten purr and purr.

Can you make other sentences using Caret U words? Read them aloud.

Here are other sentences. All members of the U family are in them. Read them aloud. Can you hear the voice of each one?

Long U   ū
Short U   ŭ
Caret U   û

Remember, each has a different sound.

1. My pup was hurt.
2. We have a fur rug.
3. We had fun with the nurse on Tuesday.
4. Use the new cup yourself.
5. We put nuts in the nut cup.
6. Have you heard the new tune?

THE KITTEN AND PUP

A kitten met a pup.
The puppy jumped up.
He said, "How do you do?
I'm glad to see you."
The kitten said, "Mew, mew!
I never really knew
How cute a pup could be
Till I saw you, you see."

We are OU and OW. We sound the same but we aren't spelled alike.

We are made from two sounds: AH (ä) and Long Double O ($\bar{oo}$).

Now make us into one sound *AH-OO*.

Be sure to sound us through the mouth and not the nose.

We are in these words. Pronounce them aloud.

now	mouse	gown	hour
vow	house	brown	mouth
bow	down	found	south
how	town	sound	flower

Can you think of other OU and OW words? Write and pronounce them.

Read these sentences aloud. Find the OU's and OW's in them.

1. Open your mouths to let out sounds.
2. "Bow-wow, bow-wow," barked Bowser.
3. I picked flowers for an hour.
4. She went downtown to buy a brown gown.
5. I heard a loud sound in the house.
6. The brown cow was lying down.
7. The mouse ran about the house.
8. I found five pounds of candy.

Make other sentences using OU and OW words. Read them aloud.

We are OI and OY.

We sound the same but we aren't spelled alike.

We are made from two sounds: AW (a̯) and Short I (ĭ).

Now make us into one sound *AW–I*.

• •

We are in these words. Pronounce them aloud.

boy	oil	joint	voice
toy	boil	point	choice
joy	soil	noise	loyal
join	coin	voyage	royal

Think of other words with OI and OY. Write and pronounce them.

Read these sentences aloud. Find the OI's and OY's in them.

1. Point to the toy.
2. Put joy in your voice.
3. The boys joined the race.
4. The boys and girls made a noise.
5. We took a voyage around the world.
6. Be loyal to your school.
7. Point to your choice.
8. The boy had a noisy toy.

Make other sentences using OI and OY words. Read them aloud.

You have been traveling THIS WAY TO
  BETTER SPEECH.
You have met sounds.
You have also met words.
You have met and made sentences.
You have enjoyed poems.
You have followed your speech guides.
You have traveled far toward Better Speech.